# AVRO LANCASTER

## Mk I & Mk III late production batches 1943-1945

## MARK POSTLETHWAITE

## Avro Lancaster Production 1943-1945

**Legend:**
- A.V. Roe (Yeadon)
- Metropolitan Vickers
- A.V. Roe (Chadderton)
- Armstrong Whitworth
- Vickers Armstrongs (Castle Bromwich)
- Austin Motors (Longbridge)
- Vickers Armstrongs (Chester)

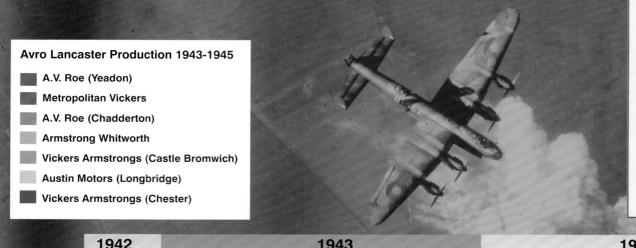

As with our previous book, we have grouped the photographs by serial batches and not chronologically. This allows the reader to spot several features that are unique to that particular batch or factory. Most major modifications and improvements were introduced chronologically and most definitely NOT by alphabetic serial numbers. As you can see below, ME551 was delivered in March 1945, nearly a year after PA964 was delivered and HK806 was delivered a full two and a half years after the later serialled LM301!

As always, there were security gaps in the serial numbers and some of the batches were finished as different Mks or as Lincolns etc, this book simply concentrates on wartime Mk Is and Mk IIIs.

| Production Batch | Approximate delivery period |
|---|---|
| HK535-HK806 | Sept 1943 – Feb 1945 |
| JA672-JB748 | May 1943 – Dec 1943 |
| LL740-LM296 | Oct 1943 – July 1944 |
| LM301-LM756 | Oct 1942 – Sept 1943 |
| ME295-ME551 | Oct 1944 – Mar 1945 |
| ME554-ME868 | Oct 1943 – July 1944 |
| ND324-NE181 | Nov 1943 – Dec 1943 |
| NF906-NG503 | May 1944 – Feb 1945 |
| NN694-NN816 | Apr 1944 – Feb 1945 |
| NX548-NX610 | Nov 1944 – Mar 1945 |
| PA158-PA509 | Oct 1944 – Sept 1945 |
| PA964-PD139 | Dec 1943 – Jan 1945 |
| PD198-PD444 | Mar 1944 – Dec 1944 |
| PP663-PP792 | Feb 1945 – Aug 1945 |
| RA500-RA805 | Dec 1944 – Apr 1945 |
| RE115-RE226 | Dec 1944 – Feb 1945 |
| RF120-RF326 | Jan 1945 – Mar 1945 |
| SW243-SW279 | Jan 1945 – Feb 1945 |

(Timeline columns run: 1942 — Oct, Nov, Dec; 1943 — Jan through Dec; 1944 — Jan through Dec; 1945 — Jan through Sept.)

Right: And to further illustrate how difficult it is to pinpoint exactly when a modification appeared on the production line, look at this line up of Lancaster cockpit sections taken in 1944. About 1/3 of them have the new larger astrodome and they are randomly placed along the line!

Below: The Lancaster was designed to be built in sections at various smaller factories and then completed at large assembly lines on airfields such as Woodford and Yeadon. Here we have brand new LM and NE series aircraft on the flight line at Woodford in May 1944. As you can see from the table opposite, the two production batches ran simultaneously, with the LM series being particularly drawn out. Another curious point about the LM series is that some were assembled at Yeadon and others at Woodford at the same time. LM570 - LM580 all came out of Yeadon apart from LM572, LM578 and LM580 which were assembled at Woodford. The Woodford examples appearing a few weeks earlier than the Yeadon siblings.

As you can see, at this time the aircraft still had needle blade propellers but had the new pitot tube position and H2S.

# MODIFICATIONS TO LOOK OUT FOR

We spilt these two books on the Mk I and Mk III into 'early production batches' and 'late production batches'. Although as you can see from the production table, one or two of these batches covered both periods, the general features for all late production batch aircraft are as follows;

No fuselage windows *except early LM and JB series aircraft.

Larger bomb aimer's blister.

Trailing aerial under the port wing.

Black painted internal framework for turrets.

Later style rear facing wingtip formation lamps.

Anti-shimmy tail wheel.

Removal of leading edge cable cutters *except early LM and JB series aircraft.

So taking ED593 (left) as a late example in the first book and RA510 (below left) as a late example in this second book, here are some of the modifications to look out for in the late production batches.

(A) Pitot tube mast. The early style pitot tube was on an angled mast on the port side of the nose, just behind the bomb-aimer's blister. The later style was mounted further back and higher up.

(B) Propellers. Needle bladed props were much thinner than the later paddle bladed props which were introduced to handle the more powerful engines.

(C) Port side cockpit blister. Generally removed with the introduction of H2S.

(D) Bomb aimer's window. The early style rectangular window was soon replaced with an oval window, initially with a rear view cupola but this was eventually removed as it proved unpopular.

(E) Rebecca Aerials. H shaped aerials added on the nose.

(F) H2S mounting frame. Added with H2S.

(G) Removal of the attachment point for the TR9 radio aerial.

(H) Removal of the navigator's window.

(J) Enlarged cockpit astrodome, a very late war mod.

(K) Window distribution box fitted on starboard side of nose.

(L) H2S and cupola fitted under the fuselage.

(M) Fuselage cabin air intake, a very late war mod.

# WINDOW

Window was small strips of aluminium foil or metal coated paper dropped by bombers to create thousands of radar echoes, which hid the echoes of the bombers themselves. This simple idea was worked out by both the Germans and the British quite early in the war, but curiously, both sides believed that using it would 'give away' the secret and allow the enemy to use it against them.  Eventually Bomber Command gained permission to use it against Hamburg in late July 1943 where it proved to be incredibly effective.  It was soon found that dropping Window from the rear fuselage flare chute was both impractical and ineffective, so a new position was found on the starboard side of the bomb-aimer's position. At first, just a small opening (A) was created on the production line, but this was occasionally extended at Base level as seen in (B), before a specifically designed 'box' (C) was applied over the original opening to encourage the scatter of the package contents.  This box appeared on most Lancasters from autumn 1943. The rare photo above right shows a 75 Squadron aircraft with an extra (non-standard) Window box (D) in the Flight Engineer's position.

# BULGED BOMB-BAY DOORS

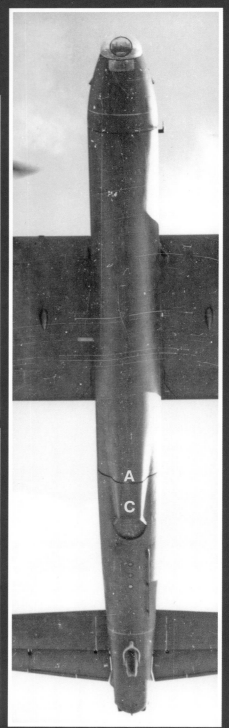

As bombs grew ever bigger, even the Lancaster's huge bomb-bay proved too small for the largest 'Cookies' such as the 12,000lb HC bomb. As such, a number of differently designed bulged bomb-bay doors were fitted to the Lancaster during its operational life. The HK series aircraft were all fitted with this type which also included an extra aft fairing (A) which was originally designed to provide a windshield for the ventral turret (B). The turret proved to be of little use so was not included in the production run, and a simple blanking plate was fitted over the hole (C).

With the introduction of upward firing cannons by the Germans in mid 1943, Bomber Command squadrons looked again at ventral armament and quite a few HK series Lancasters were fitted with a .5 machine gun in the empty turret space, using the bulged bomb bay fairing (D) as a useful windshield. (See page 9) Results were not favourable however, a 5 Group bulletin reported that;

*"With the gunner strapped in his seat it is difficult to follow the gun round on the beam; it is difficult for the gunner to get his head down behind the sight as it tends to push the oxygen mask upwards on the gunner's face; and also considerable vibration is experienced on the sight when the gun is fired"*

The most recognisable feature of the HK series of Lancaster was the bulged bomb-bay doors (A) with the extended fairing (B) which would have formed a streamlined cover for the deleted mid under turret. HK593 JN-X is from 75 Squadron's 'C' Flight. The squadron had the unusual habit of painting the JN codes aft of the roundel on the port side, which covered the HK part of the serial number. They therefore repainted the HK letters above the three digits as can be seen (arrowed).

Note the later position for the pitot tube (C) and lack of observation blister on the port side of the cockpit for this aircraft delivered in late July 1944.

Below: HK554 JN-F lost both ailerons during violent evasive action over Russelheim on 26 August 1944. Being one of the earliest in the HK series, it was delivered in May 1944 with the early positioned pitot tube (A). Once again, the JN codes have covered the HK part of the original serial number.

Right: The crew of HK545 of 115 Squadron climb aboard, note the 'clover leaf' gas detection patch (arrowed) just in front of the rear turret, a common sight on 3 Group Lancasters. Note the very early examples in the HK series appear to have had fuselage windows fitted but overpainted.

Main photo: Another squadron that had its fair share of HK series Lancasters was 622 based at Mildenhall. This one, GI-Z HK615, was one of several on the squadron that had a .5 calibre machine gun fitted into the vacant lower turret area. This aircraft also appears to be fitted with Monica Mk.V, (see page 56), note the double headed aerial (A) under the rear turret and two faintly visible vertical aerials (B) on the starboard wing. Again no observation blister is present on the port side of the cockpit.

Inset below: This rare photo actually shows the gun in position (arrowed). Although often captioned as having a different serial number in other publications, GI-B is undoubtedly HK651 of 622 Squadron.

Right: A closer view of the extended bomb bay rear fairing. This aircraft, HK692 is a 138 Squadron example seen here whilst ferrying former POWs back to the UK. The chalked graffiti was quite common during this operation!

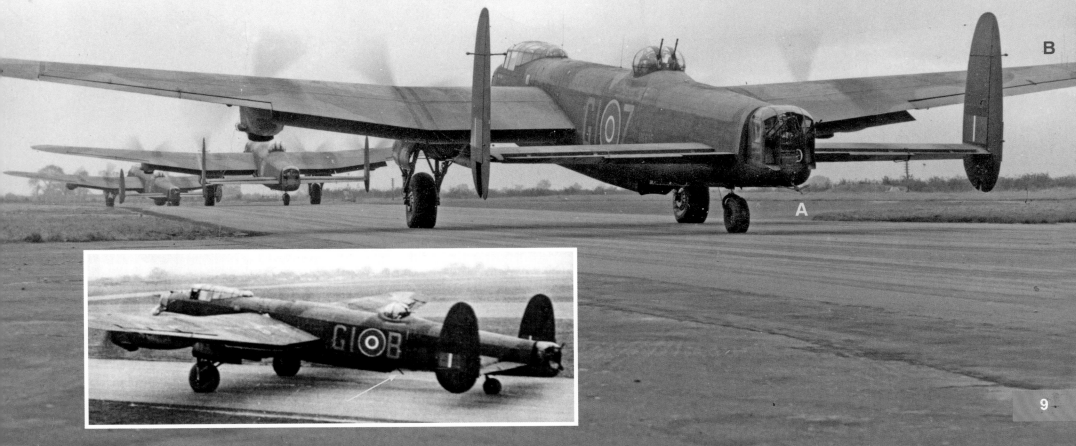

**Left:** HK798 was one of the last of the HK series to be delivered, in February 1945, seen here with 115 Squadron's 'C' Flight. Just visible is the tall astrodome (A) at the rear of the cockpit, a late war modification.

**Below:** Another late example HK795 of 149 Squadron's 'C' Flight also carries the enlarged astrodome (arrowed). It also has a 'clover leaf' gas detection patch just forward of the mid-upper turret and G-H Leader yellow stripes* on the fins, (*see page 21). From photographic evidence, it appears that most of the HK series had needle blade props and only a few received the later paddle bladed versions, probably because most HKs were delivered with Merlin 22s.

Both aircraft on this page were fitted with Merlin 24s.

A.V. Roe Chadderton

350 Lancaster Mk Is

Serial Range

## JA672 – JB748

June 43 – Dec 43

We covered the early examples of this batch in the previous book so here are later JB serialled examples.

Inset: JB375 joined the TFU at Defford in October 1943 to test equipment such as Monica Mk III (A) and Village Inn (B) and H2S (C).

Main photo: This is JB607 of 460 Squadron fitted with H2S (arrowed), although partially obscured by the censor. The fitting of H2S and deletion of fuselage windows was applied mid-way through this batch of serials. Note the radiator vents (A) are in the fully open position to keep the engines cool during taxiing.

11

Lancaster JB743 CF-C is an ex-460 Squadron aircraft now seen here at Mount Farm with 625 Squadron in June 1944. The large circular patch on the nose is a yellow gas detection device that was carried by many 1 Group aircraft, (see page 14). Interestingly, and unusually, it carries another patch on the rear entrance door (arrowed). This aircraft was shot down shortly after this photo was taken, on 1st July 1944. Note the overpainted AR codes of 460 Squadron in the inset photo.

# LANCASTER Mk III JB743 CF-C 625 SQUADRON (JUNE 1944)

## Modeller's notes

Very late JB series aircraft, delivered to 460 Sqn December 1943
Transferred to 625 Sqn 13.6.44

No fuselage windows
Needle blade props
Z-Equipment rings in bomb aimer's blister
Early pitot tube
H2S
Oval bomb aimer's window with cupola
No port cockpit blister
Monica aerial
Gas detection patches on both nose and door
One landing light
Overpainted AR codes of 460 Squadron
Nose-Art is Captain A. R. P. Reilly-Foull saying 'Stap Me'

Shot down 1 July 1944

Right: 'Captain' stands next to an invasion striped USAAF A20 at Mount Farm.

# GAS DETECTION PATCHES

Gas detection patches, usually light yellow/green in colour, were applied to most RAF aircraft at the beginning of WW2 as the fear of gas attack was very high. These patches would turn a different colour when exposed to poisonous gas and would therefore alert crews and groundcrews accordingly. By 1941 the threat was all but gone and the patches disappeared from most RAF aircraft. The Lancasters of 1 Group and 3 Group were an exception, with most 1 Group aircraft carrying the large circular patch and 3 Group aircraft having 'clover leaf' patches on the upper fuselage. The reason is believed to be that these two Groups were designated to be the ones to drop chemical weapons should the war escalate to that extreme.

Clockwise from the top;

A rare colour photo of a 100 Squadron Lanc (1 Group)

A lower position for the circle on this 12 Sqn Lanc, (1 Group)

A stained patch on TC-E of 170 Sqn (1 Group)

LS-H has the clover leaf patch near the turret (3 Group)

Armstrong Whitworth
350 Lancaster Mk Is

Serial Range

**LL740 – LM296**

Nov 43 – Aug 44

Left: LL744 VN-B of 50 Squadron at Skellingthorpe in January 1944. Only the very early of this batch had needle bladed props like this one.

Below: LL783 PG-C of 619 Squadron provides a fine study of the undersides. Points of interest include the circular mid-under gun turret blanking plate (A) which sits proud of the curve of the fuselage, and the new oval shaped bomb-aimer's window with the transparent cupola (B) which was open at the rear and allowed the bomb-aimer to look back underneath the bomber's fuselage.

Left: LL806 holds the joint record with ED888 as having flown the most operational sorties by any Lancaster at 140. It joined XV Squadron in April 1944 and survived the war, as shown here wearing the post war white codes and underwing serial numbers. The exhaust shrouds have been removed now that night bombing missions were not being flown.

Bottom left: LL842 VN-F of 50 Squadron shows that paddle bladed props were soon introduced on this production batch. This photo was taken in May 1944 and the aircraft was shot down on 24/25 July 1944. The paddle bladed props were introduced to handle the greater power of the improved Merlin engines being fitted in 1944 such as the Merlin 24. There were initial problems linked with the old constant speed units which led to overspeeding and engine disintegration, but this was soon fixed with modified CSUs.

Below: A newly delivered LL779 still carries the chalk marks for the 101 Squadron codes. Note how the squadron has removed the factory applied roundel (A) and repainted it further back to provide room for the SR codes forward of the roundel. Just visible on top of the fuselage is an ABC aerial (B) and just visible in the open door is the larger set of flare tubes (C) mounted on the port side of the fuselage (see page 68)

Right: LL849 UM-B$^2$ of 626 Squadron after being stuck by lightning on the infamous Nuremberg Raid of 31 March 1944.

Below: LL964 AR-D of 460 Squadron RAAF photographed in July 1944. Additional features on this airframe are; (A) squadron fitted extensions to the exhaust shrouds, (B) Window dispersal box (deleted by the censor), (C) Z equipment rings in the bomb aimer's blister (see page 80). This squadron was in 1 Group so the large gas patch is carried on the nose.

LL966 LE-P of 630 Squadron photographed at East Kirkby in summer 1944. The yellow outlined codes and coloured fin markings are typical 5 Group features during this period of daylight raids. 'Prune's Pride' is painted on the nose along with a small drawing of Pilot Officer Prune.

# LANCASTER Mk I LL966 LE-P 630 SQUADRON (SUMMER 1944)

## Modeller's notes

Delivered to 630 Squadron 6 May 1944

No fuselage windows
Paddle blade props
Z-Equipment rings in bomb aimer's blister
Early pitot tube
H2S
Oval bomb aimer's window with rear view cupola
No port cockpit blister
Daylight fin markings black stripe on red
Codes outlined in yellow
Unpainted wheel hubs

Nose art 'Prune's Pride' possibly in yellow or white with a faint
drawing of Pilot Officer Prune
Letter P in a square behind bomb aimer's side window

Shot down 15 February 1945

Right: Another 630 Squadron Lancaster LM287 showing a
different form of fin marking which backs up the theory that
the markings were quite 'unofficial' and applied at unit level.

Above: LM239 PO-M of 467 Squadron photographed in the summer of 1944. During this period, 5 Group was flying a lot of daylight sorties and had introduced informal quick recognition markings such as coloured fins and highlighted code letters as seen here.

Above right: This photo of LM287 LE-O of 630 Squadron is interesting because the blurred line running diagonally across the picture is the old IFF aerial wire running from fin to fuselage. These Lancasters carried the later IFF Mk III rod aerial under the fuselage but these wires for the Mk II system appear to have been retained and possibly re-purposed.

Right: LM257 HA-P of 218 Squadron photographed on 4 December 1944. Of interest in this photo is that LM257 is fitted with the later style pitot tube (arrowed). The two stripes on the fin indicate a Gee-H leader, (see opposite page).

Gee-H or (G-H) was a radio navigation system used to guide bombers to their targets. It was developed from the earlier Gee navigational system which used radio pulses sent from ground stations to measure the distances away from them and thus determine the position of the aircraft.

Gee-H was first used in November 1943 but could only be used by less than 100 aircraft on any one raid due to the capacity of the ground stations to handle the signals from the individual aircraft. As such, just 3 Group was designated to operate Gee-H and when daylight raids were launched in 1944, the Group issued orders to paint two horizontal white (quickly changed to yellow) bars on the fins of the Lancasters carrying the equipment. The procedure would then be for at least two non-equipped aircraft to formate on the Gee-H marked aircraft and bomb when they did.

Above: NG358 LS-H of XV Squadron clearly displays its Gee-H bars, note the larger astrodome fitted to the last of the NG series aircraft.

Left: Another 3 Group squadron was 622 carrying GI codes. Again the Gee-H bars are very visible.

A.V. Roe Yeadon

350 Lancaster Mk IIIs*

Serial Range

**LM301 – LM756**

Oct 42 – Oct 44

*First 10 as Mk Is

This batch of Lancasters took an incredible two years to complete, so there are plenty of differences between the early and late examples, the most significant being the fuselage windows. These two early examples on this page clearly show the windows which were discontinued somewhere between LM372 and LM418.

Top right: EM-Z of 207 Squadron is LM326 seen here in mid-1943 very much looking like an early production Lancaster with a full set of windows and an observation blister in the port side of the cockpit.

Right: LM360 QR-O is the aircraft that Bill Reid brought back from Düsseldorf on the night of 3 November 1943, subsequently being awarded the VC for his actions that night. This photo was taken at Shipdham the morning after, showing the extent of the damage inflicted by the attacking night fighters. Reid was badly injured during the combat but survived, his navigator and wireless operator both died.

This is Reg Welham and his crew in front of LM393 UM-W² of 626 Squadron, photographed on 27 January 1944. The two holes (A) in the leading edge are to supply air inwards through a radiator to heat the fuselage. The two vents (B) are to allow the circulated air to escape. The little slot (arrowed) in the pitot tube mast is a thermometer to measure air temperature. Note the early style rectangular bomb aimer's window.

Also visible in this photo are the leading edge cable cutters (C) which were not carried by most late production aircraft.

B

B

C C
A

C C
A

Above: One of the finest wartime Lancaster photos ever taken shows LM418 PG-S of 619 Squadron on 14 February 1944. Clearly by this airframe, the fuselage windows had been deleted on the production line. Note the two auxiliary air intakes are on the inboard engines only, the port one being larger than the starboard. The small vent (A) is the first attempt at a specific Window dispersal point, as opposed to using the flare chute, see page 5 for more details.

Left: Another photo taken that day showing LM449 PG-H again with no fuselage windows apart from the wireless operator's big square window under the astrodome. Also note the port observation blister on the cockpit canopy has been deleted.

Below: Often mistakenly captioned as LM449 PG-H (seen in the inset opposite) this is actually LL783 PG-C, (also seen on page 15). The key difference is the Mandrel aerial (A) which is offset to the side and kinked downwards. On both aircraft opposite it is mounted vertically under the fuselage. This is because the LM series aircraft had the old rectangular bomb-aimer's window underneath, whereas the LL series had the longer oval window with the clear blister (B) which occupied the space needed to mount the aerial. The inset photo (right) shows a similar solution on ND578.

# AERIALS

Left: LM522 photographed in the Avro assembly shop at Yeadon circa February 1943. This airframe was the first to be fitted with H2S on the production line.

Below inset: LM482 KC-W of 617 Squadron was the regular mount of Dambuster Les Munro. One of the last 'LM's to be delivered without H2S, the aircraft has been fitted with bulged bomb doors for 617's specialist bombing role.

Bottom: Now with H2S, LM583 of 467 Squadron has Z equipment rings fitted in the bomb aimer's blister, dating the picture to late June/July 1944 as the aircraft was lost at the end of the July. The white tail with blue cross is a 5 Group daylight formation marking.

H2S was a ground scanning radar that was developed to find bombing targets at night and through cloud. It was tested in action by Pathfinders in early 1943 and it soon became clear that it could also be used as a navigation aid. It was hoped to equip every Lancaster with this aid as standard, especially as it was also found to be able to detect night fighters underneath the bomber. (This involved the use of a separate display unit in the Wireless Operator's position codenamed Fishpond.)

Originally, the bomb aimer would sit next to the navigator to operate H2S to ease his workload, but as H2S sets became more advanced, the navigator tended to simply refer to the H2S as and when he needed it.

In summer 1944, its use was restricted after the RAF discovered that German night fighters were homing in on H2S signals but improvements and only essential periods of use enabled the bombers to keep using it until the end of the war.

Above: The equipment was mounted at the forward end of the navigator's table on a metal framework which took up most of the space behind the pilot's seat.

Top right: The rear half of the fairing was usually left unpainted to allow the downward identification light (arrowed) to be seen.

Middle right: A Wireless Operator using the Fishpond equipment.

Bottom right: The rotating scanner was enclosed in a Perspex fairing in the redundant lower gun position.

Main photo: LM577 of 218 Squadron shows the H2S mounting pole (A) that was fitted inside the cockpit to allow the set to swivel on the end of the navigator's desk. (B) is a bracket to secure it to the cockpit framing.

Inset: The mounting pole and frame seen before the installation of the H2S set, (A) is the pole seen in the main photo.

Main photo and left: LM630 PG-D 'Dumbo' photographed on a winter's day in late 1944/early 1945. It has 63 ops recorded on the side of the nose and yellow outlines to the squadron codes, introduced in summer 1944. The aircraft has the late style pitot tube but old style needle blade props.

Below left: LM732 TC-C of 170 Squadron has all the standard features of the late LM series but carries a very non-standard Rose rear turret, see page 30.

# THE ROSE TURRET

Soon after the Lancaster entered service, it was already clear that the .303 machine gun defensive armament was weak compared to the German fighters' 20mm cannons. With official committees taking forever to agree a solution, Arthur Harris himself asked Rose Brothers in Gainsborough to design an improved rear turret for his Lancaster force.  The result was the Rose-Rice turret as seen here, fitted with two 0.5 inch heavy machine guns. It was a big improvement although it suffered more stoppages than the standard FN turret.  By the end of the war, less that 200 turrets had been retro-fitted to Lancasters, mainly from 1 Group which was based near the Gainsborough factory.

Above: One major improvement was the gunner's ability to bale out directly in front of him.

Above right: The turret was open to the elements for better visibility, and was found to be only 4 degrees colder than an enclosed turret.

Right: Two gunners emphasise the increase in space inside the Rose turret.

A.V. Roe Yeadon

200 Lancaster Mk I & IIIs

Serial Range

## ME295 – ME551

Oct 44 – Mar 45

This comparatively small batch of Lancasters followed the previous batch at A.V. Roe's Yeadon factory, so didn't start deliveries until October 1944. As such, they all had the late war features such as large astrodome (A), Rebecca aerials (B), Z rings (C), fuselage air intake (D), Window box (E), late pitot tube (F) and paddle blade props (G).

Top left is ME470 of 300 (Polish) Squadron.

Above is ME520 of 97 Squadron post-war showing the underwing serials.

Left is ME536 AL-Q of 429 Squadron RCAF at Pomigliano in Italy during Operation Dodge, the repatriation of thousands of Allied troops back to the UK from Italy.

The first of this batch of Lancasters was delivered almost a year before the previous batch so they still had the old position pitot tube and smaller astrodome.

Right: ME562 is KC-K of 617 Squadron, seen here with F/O Sanders and his crew after sinking the Tirpitz on 12 November 1944. This raid was flown at extremely long range and so the mid-upper turret was removed to save weight.

Below: AR-J$^2$ of 460 Squadron RAAF is ME649 photographed in summer 1944.

ME746 AS-R² of 166 Squadron is seen here being awarded an honorary DSO after flying its 100th op on 11 March 1945. Observable features of the batch are deleted port observation blister in the cockpit, oval bomb aimer's window but without the rear view cupola, old style pitot tube and paddle blade props.

ME701 JO-F of 463 Squadron on a dispersal pan probably at Waddington in spring 1944. The early ME series aircraft had Merlin 22s and probably needle blade props, but from ME640 in early February 1944 Merlin 24s were fitted along with paddle blade props as seen here. Note the heavy oil leaks from the spinners and nacelles indicating the initial problems with the paddle blade props and the constant speed units.

Of interest is the towing attachment fitted to the small lugs under the rear fuselage. These mysterious little lugs behind the tail wheel appear on many Lancaster photos and can be seen arrowed in the top inset photo.

# LANCASTER Mk I ME701 JO-F 463 SQUADRON (SPRING 1944)

## Modeller's notes

Delivered to 463 Squadron 19 March 1944

Merlin 24 engines
No fuselage windows
Paddle blade props
Early pitot tube
H2S
Oval bomb aimer's window
No port cockpit blister
Painted wheel hubs
Significant oil leaks from spinners relating to CSU problems
with the new paddle blade props
Monica aerial possibly carried at some point

Nose art 'Whoa Bessie'

Damaged beyond repair 2 July 1944

Right: A close up of the nose of ME701 with pilot Flt Lt B A
Buckham DSO DFC in the cockpit.

Left: ME844 was delivered to XV Squadron in June 1944 and coded LS-C.

Below left and below: A year later and the same aircraft now coded LS-W with all code letters now repainted in a white script style. The uppersurface camouflage scheme changed little throughout the operational life of the Lancaster. Note that this airframe has the later style pitot tube, possibly retro-fitted but more likely introduced late on the 'ME' production line.

The exhausts shrouds are visible in the wartime photo but were easily removed when not needed, as seen in the lower photos.

600 Lancasters were built in this batch in a comparatively short period of time. This aircraft is ND458 HW-A 'Able Mabel' of 100 Squadron which went on to complete 134 operational sorties. Note the extended exhaust dampers (A), usually fitted at squadron level within 1 Group. Also note the port side cockpit blister (arrowed) which doesn't appear on later ND series aircraft. The H2S framework is visible inside the cockpit (next to the arrow) which means that it would be pretty impossible to gain access to the blister, which is why it was soon deleted.

A.V. Roe (Chadderton)
600 Lancaster Mk IIIs
Serial Range

**ND324 – NE181**

Dec 43 – May 44

ND521 UL-L² looking a bit forlorn after a partial undercarriage collapse on 18 November 1944. It had already been significantly damaged with 207 Squadron in March and went through various repair units before being re-issued to 576 on 27 September. It must have been during the repair process that the aircraft was upgraded to paddle blade props as later ND serialled aircraft continued to have needle bladed props. It also received Rebecca aerials, again not standard for this production batch.

Right: ND591 OL-A of 97 Squadron seen on display to the public post-war.

Below: ND619 CF-D 'Dagwood' of 625 Squadron after making an emergency landing at Mount Farm in July 1944 with an injured pilot. Close examination of the cockpit area shows a bullet hole (arrowed) in the bomb tally which probably caused the injury.

ND644 HW-N was another centurion that flew with 100 Squadron from February 1944. It too has the extended exhaust shrouds and the usual 1 Group gas patch prominent on the nose. What is different is the later pitot tube position, presumably added on the production line mid-batch. Still in place is the rear view cupola (arrowed) under the bomb-aimer's position.

Top: This unidentified Lancaster shows a little known modification carried out by a few squadrons in spring 1944. The night bombing offensive was at its peak and the nose turret was useless at night, so the turret was removed and faired over to save weight. This was particularly noted amongst Pathfinder squadrons.

Above: ND759 TL-R of 35 Squadron was another Lancaster modified in this way. It force landed on a lake in Switzerland on 28 April 1944 and remained there for 10 years before being salvaged. The blanked nose turret is clearly visible. By June 1944, daylight operations were being flown once again and the missing nose turrets were hastily reinstalled.

Right: NE181, the final Lancaster in this production batch, also achieved 100 operations as JN-M 'The Captain's Fancy'. The bomb aimer's rear view cupola has been replaced by a flat oval perspex panel (arrowed). Many bomb aimers found it very uncomfortable to use the cupola as it involved poking their head through the hole and looking upside down backwards; a sure recipe for air-sickness! The presence of needle blade props confirms that the entire production batch had them.

The main new feature about this production batch is the introduction of Rebecca aerials on the nose. These early examples seem to have had the forward half of the aerials painted white or in natural metal.

Left: NF926 of 218 Squadron is seen here taking off on 4 December 1944, it was shot down some three weeks later.

Below: NF971 of 149 Squadron photographed through an amber or red filter to make the sky darker and more dramatic. This filter also lightens the codes and the red in the roundel.

Left: KC-B is NG494 of 617 Squadron. Again, the 'Dambusters' have modified their aircraft to suit their needs by removing the H2S and adding bulged bomb doors. Note the enlarged astrodome which is probably a production line feature.

Below: NG162 is A4-W 'Willie the Conk' (William the Conqueror) of 195 Squadron. This aircraft has the standard sized astrodome so the larger version must have been introduced soon after this airframe.

# REBECCA

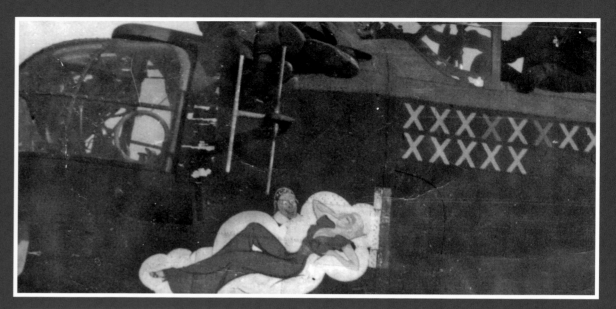

The H shaped 'Rebecca' aerials that appeared on the production line in mid-1944 were essentially part of a homing system that helped the pilot find a runway in poor weather. Originally designed as a homing system to drop supplies to agents on the ground equipped with a 'Eureka' transmitter, it was realised that if these ground based transmitters were placed at the end of Bomber Command runways, it could also help guide aircraft down to land. The runway transmitters were codenamed BABS and the system remained in use long after the war ended.

The photo (right) clearly shows the light coloured forward aerial and stem of the early examples, seen here on NG287.

NG347 QB-P 'Piccadilly Princess' of 424 (Tiger) Squadron photographed in spring 1945. The Canadian squadrons were known for their nose art and this one is particularly impressive! Just visible is the larger astrodome. Note the lack of exhaust residue and the missing exhaust shrouds.

424 Squadron only converted to Lancasters in January 1945 and NG347 was one of the first to arrive. The Canadian squadrons painted some of the largest nose art seen on Lancasters and Piccadilly Princess is a prime example. Of interest is the Lorenz 'towel rail' aerial (arrowed) still fitted despite the Rebecca aerials now in place on the nose.

# LANCASTER Mk I NG347 QB-P 424 SQUADRON (EARLY 1945)

## Modeller's notes

Delivered to 424 Squadron 24 January 1945

Merlin 24 engines
No fuselage windows
Paddle blade props
Late pitot tube
H2S
Oval bomb aimer's window
No port cockpit blister
Z Equipment rings
Large astrodome
Window box
Rebecca Aerials
Lorenz 'towel rail' aerial

Nose art 'Piccadilly Princess' with large 'Varga' girl artwork
Possibly three medal ribbons under the text.

Survived the war

Just 100 aircraft in this batch which took new manufacturer Austin Motors nearly a year to complete.

Left: NN742 of 150 Squadron over Lincoln Cathedral.

Below left: NN692 showing the early style pitot tube.

Below: NN748 of 300 Squadron, note the white marks applied to the tail wheel tyre and rim to check for any displacement between the two.

The second batch built by Austin was a rare group of Mk Is which were Mk VII interims. In other words, there were Mk VII features already in this batch such as the re-positioned mid-upper turret.

Right: This rare photo shows one of these 50 Lancasters, NX565, with 12 Squadron, fitted with the standard FN50 in a non standard forward position.

Below: After NX610 the production turned to Mk VII (FE) variants like this one which will be featured in a future book.

Austin Motors
50 Lancaster Mk Is
Serial Range
NX548 – NX610
Feb 45 – April 45

Another batch that took over a year to complete with anything after PA335 being post-war and out of the scope of this book.

Above: PA170 of XV Squadron lines up for take off, flaps 20, radiator shutters fully open, guns in turrets pointing skywards to avoid accidents during taxiing.

Right: The same aircraft at Juvincourt on 4 December 1944 with a hefty chunk out of its starboard fin. Note the paddle blade props.

Top left: The crew of PA168 P4-G provide us with a detailed view of the whip aerials on the fuselage. Note how the internal canopy frames are painted or taped from the outside.

Left: PA238 SR-Z of 101 Squadron takes off from Pomigliano, Italy during Operation Dodge. Being 1 Group, the circular gas patch is still there although the exhaust shrouds are not. It appears to have the early small astrodome which would soon be replaced on the production line by the large version, (PA266 had the large astrodome).

Above: Just to emphasise how chronologically out of sequence the late PA series were, PA386 first appeared in June 1945 and has all the late and post-war mods including the FN82 twin machine gun rear turret and larger rudders (arrowed). This rudder extension can be seen on the BBMF's PA474 and is often described as a 'Lincoln' rudder, but as you can see here, the extension was an original feature of this batch of late PA series aircraft.

This is the largest single batch of Lancasters, so plenty of upgrades are visible throughout the production run.

Above: The first aircraft was PA964, delivered in May 1944 and seen here with 7 Squadron as MG-K. Production features at this stage include, needle blade props, rear view cupola, late position pitot tube, Window box and H2S. This aircraft also has a Boozer aerial (arrowed) above the rear turret, (see opposite page).

Left: PB139 XY-C 'The Commando' of 186 Squadron confirms the later position pitot tube.

# BOOZER

Boozer was the code name for a vertically mounted aerial positioned above the rear turret, which detected when an enemy aircraft's radar was illuminating the bomber. First trialled in 1942, it was linked to two lamps in front of the pilot which would light up when Boozer detected radar signals hitting the aircraft. Boozer was further developed with an additional downward facing aerial to detect ground based Würzburg radar signals as well. The lamps in the cockpit then displayed two different colours, yellow and red, depending upon whether it was detecting a fighter radar or ground based radar.

Generally, Boozer didn't perform particularly well and it was overtaken by devices such as Visual Monica and Village Inn which helped the crews locate the approaching fighter as well as detecting it, even if it wasn't using radar.

Right and below: At a very bleak looking Binbrook is PB383 AR- H² of 460 Squadron. This is a very rare photo as it depicts an operational Lancaster fitted with both Monica Mk III and Village Inn. Although the mast above the rear turret looks like a Boozer aerial, the hoizontal aerials show that it's 'Visual Monica'. All early features of this production run are still present including needle blade props etc.

Inset right: Another 460 Squadron aircraft AR-U, probably PB407, also fitted with the Village Inn and Monica Mk III combination.

# MONICA Mk III (VISUAL MONICA)

The original Monica tail warning radar (above), introduced in summer 1942, was a simple transmitter and receiver that detected aircraft behind the bomber and alerted the crew by audible blips in the intercom system.

Monica Mk III (Visual Monica) was a more sophisticated version that produced the blips but also a visual display for the Wireless Operator who was able to determine the range and approximate position of the unidentified aircraft and guide the rear gunner in his search. When combined with 'Village Inn' (see page 79) the gunner could then use the radar equipped turret to acquire the target aircraft and engage it.

This technology was introduced in early 1944 and was proving to be very useful, but in July 1944 a captured German night fighter was found to have equipment that homed in on Monica's transmissions and orders went out to all squadrons to cease the use of Monica immediately, pending a solution.

Top left: The receiving aerials for Monica Mk III mounted on the tail fin. Top right: The Monica Mk III transmitting aerial with the extra horizontal rod. This is seen here mounted above the turret to allow Village Inn to be fitted. It is believed that without Village Inn, the aerial was mounted underneath the rear turret like the original Monica aerial.

Bottom left: Monica Mk III mounted above a Village Inn equipped turret, the aerial (A) may be an alternative position for the fin mounted receivers. Bottom right: A Wireless Operator using the Visual Monica set.

# MONICA Mk V

Monica Mk V (Lulu) was a further development of the tail warning radar idea, this time using surplus Al Mk IV radar sets from night fighters, but mounted backwards instead of forwards. The main double chevron transmitting aerial (A) was mounted under the rear turret and the receiving aerials (B) were mounted above and below the starboard wing. Again, the Wireless Operator had a visual display which he monitored and passed instructions back to the rear gunner.

Only around 300 sets were installed, scattered between several squadrons, but 5 Group reported positive results in the spring and summer of 1944. As with Monica Mk III, this came to an end in August 1944 when it was discovered that German fighters were homing in on the transmissions.

Above: W/O Jimmy Huck of 61 Squadron after shooting down an Me262.

Top right: A 622 Squadron Lancaster clearly fitted with Monica Mk V

Middle right: PD238 KC-H of 617 Squadron is also fitted with Monica Mk V

Bottom right: A close up of the wing aerials of Monica Mk V.

Top: PB306 PO-J of 467 Squadron RAAF displaying typical summer 1944 5 Group markings of yellow outlined codes and individual code repeated on the fin.

Above: A close up of the thinly outlined code on PB754.

Right: PB410 OF-J of 97 Squadron also carries yellow outlined fuselage codes as well as the codes being repeated on the tailplane. The weathering is very impressive and confirms the 'rule' that the outboard engines only had one exhaust streak on the uppersurfaces as the outboard exhaust gases flowed under the wing.

PB410 is typical of a hard working Lancaster in the summer/autumn 1944. Codes are outlined in yellow and repeated on the tailplane for daylight ops, and the uppersurfaces are very weathered with replacement panels giving the upper wing roundels a very odd appearance. A very rare extension to the original flare tube can be seen (arrowed). This might be connected to 97 Squadron being a Pathfinder squadron and needing to release flares from this old chute safely past the newly installed H2S cupola. The cupola itself is unusual, being painted black completely rather than having the rear section left clear.

# LANCASTER Mk III PB410 OF-J 97 SQUADRON (AUTUMN 1944)

## Modeller's notes

Delivered to 97 Squadron in August 1944

Merlin 38 engines
No fuselage windows
Needle blade props
Late pitot tube
H2S
Oval bomb aimer's window
No port cockpit blister
Z Equipment rings
Large astrodome
Rebecca Aerials
Extension to the old flare tube position
Completely black painted H2S cupola

Typical small sized 97 Squadron codes outlined in yellow and
repeated on the tailplane upper surfaces.
White (?) spinner tips on outboard engines.

Survived the war

Right: Demonstrating flying on just the two starboard engines, this
photo also highlights the light coloured tip to the outer spinners.

The two photos on these pages show significant variations in the lettering style of the serial number and the dinghy release warning signs. This is probably because some of this batch were constructed at Yeadon instead of Chadderton and PB422 was a Mk III whereas PB739 was a Mk I.

PB422 is seen here with 97 Squadron during Operation Exodus bringing clearly happy POWs back home to the UK.

The rectangular plate (arrowed) seen on all Lancasters is the static port. This was a small hole which measured the normal or 'static' air pressure which could then be compared to the pressure from the pitot tube to provide data for the air speed indicator.

PB739 of 50 Squadron has a very unusual hyphen in its serial number. The external dinghy release handle was a common feature along with an internal release cord in the fuselage. There was also an automatic immersion switch that released the dinghy when in contact with water.

Top left: PB437 of 7 Squadron is another aircraft engaged in Operation Exodus, note the now obligatory chalked graffiti!

Top right: A year later and PB437 was now coded A3-P at 1653 HCU with white painted codes and even the fuselage serial in white. Note the coloured spinners and a new FN82 rear turret.

Left: PB509 is OJ-C of 149 Squadron, seen here in early 1945. It was delivered in August 1944 so still has the smaller astrodome and possibly needle bladed props.

Above: Just visible in this photo of PB736 CF-C of 625 Squadron is the later style astrodome. This aircraft was one of the Mk Is in this batch, delivered in late October 1944.

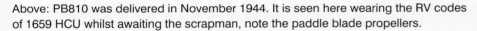

Above: PB810 was delivered in November 1944. It is seen here wearing the RV codes of 1659 HCU whilst awaiting the scrapman, note the paddle blade propellers.

Above right: PB935 of 635 Squadron photographed at Lübeck during Operation Exodus. Note the tall astrodome and the cabin air intake added to these late examples.

Below: Also photographed at Lübeck is PB979, another 635 Squadron aircraft, fitted with a FN121 'Village Inn' equipped rear turret.

# AIR TO AIR REFUELLING TRIALS

In 1944, plans were already being made for sending RAF Bomber Command heavy bombers to the Far East to bomb Japan. At the time, no Allied bases were close enough to Japan to facilitate this, so research was commenced into an air to air refuelling option. Using techniques developed before the war, Lancaster PB972 (seen here) was converted into a tanker aircraft with ND648 being modified as a receiver aircraft.

Trials began in early 1945 out of Staverton and were generally successful. By that time however, the Allies had advanced in the Pacific to the point where they now had bases within range of Japan, and so the project was cancelled.

Far left: PB972 trailing the refuelling hose from the rear of the bomb bay. The two small aerials (arrowed) are transmitter aerials for the Rebecca/Eureka system, not commonly fitted to bomber versions.

Above left: A view from the rear of the bomb bay forwards showing the refuelling hose and extra fuel tanks.

Middle left: Unlike modern trailing air to air refuelling techniques, this system fired a hook and cable sideways to engage the receiver's cable using this apparatus.

Left: PB972 being prepared for flight. (A) is a specially installed observation blister for the hose operator, (B) is the position of the hook and cable gun seen middle left.

Another experimental aircraft, PB995 was converted to carry the 22,000lb Grand Slam bomb and was used extensively for trials. All subsequent aircraft in this batch became B.1 Specials to carry this huge weapon and will be covered in a future book.

At this point, the mid-upper turret and nose turrets were retained, but these would be removed to save weight on the following examples. The removal of the Rebecca aerials is interesting however.

A straightforward batch of late Lancasters with all mods apart from the enlarged astrodome and fuselage air intake.

Top right: PD217 of 207 Squadron after a mid air collision on 12/13 September 1944, confirming paddle blade props on this batch.

Main photo: PD235 UL-N2 of 576 Squadron on an unarmed air test shortly after delivery in August 1944. Note the lack of exhaust stains and how all four engine cowling tops are in the Dark Earth colour. The two dark circles (arrowed) are windows in the two fuselage escape hatches

Two more views of PD235 showing some nice close up details including the cut-off rear tip of the H2S cupola (A) and the small inspection window in the dinghy stowage (B).

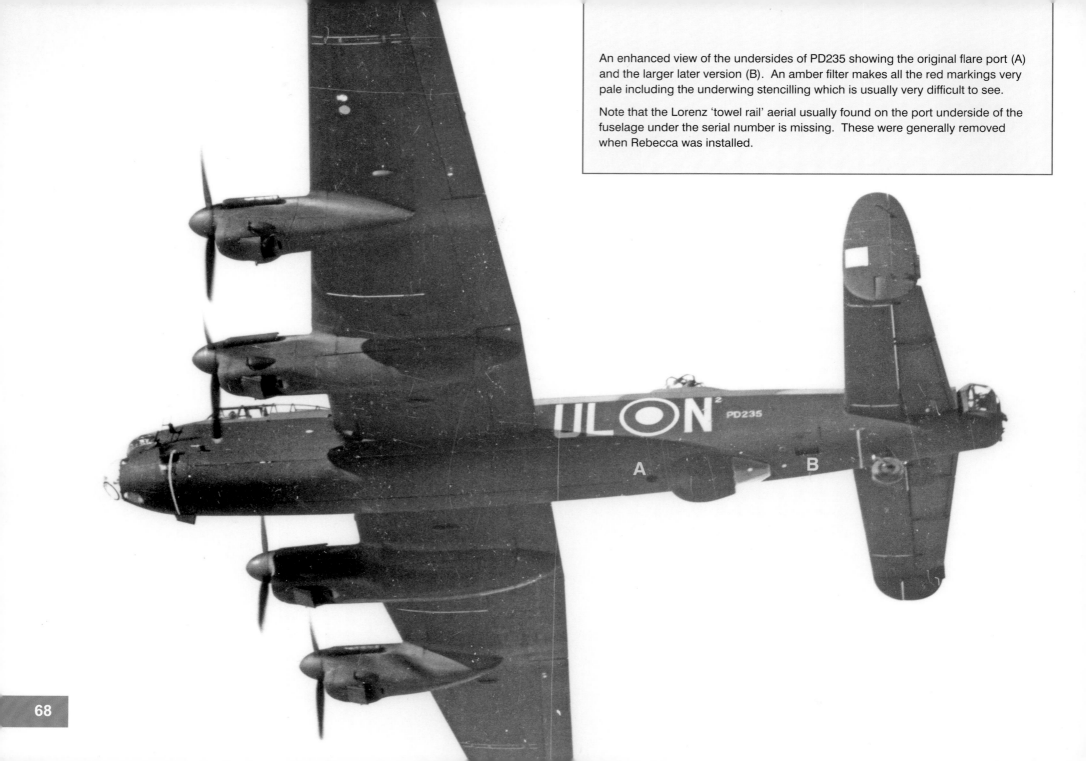

An enhanced view of the undersides of PD235 showing the original flare port (A) and the larger later version (B). An amber filter makes all the red markings very pale including the underwing stencilling which is usually very difficult to see.

Note that the Lorenz 'towel rail' aerial usually found on the port underside of the fuselage under the serial number is missing. These were generally removed when Rebecca was installed.

Below: PD336 WP-P of 90 Squadron after an air to air collision with another 90 Squadron Lancaster, HK610 WP-Z on 2/3 February 1945. As usual, the 3 Group clover leaf gas detection patch is visible forward of the mid-upper turret.

Right: Just over two weeks later, PD336 took a direct flak hit and exploded during a daylight raid, all on board including the Squadron C/O were killed instantly.

Left: PD223 of 218 Squadron is interesting as it clearly still has the old Lorenz 'towel rail' SBA aerial (arrowed) under the fuselage. Note also the 'clover leaf' gas patch in front of the mid-upper turret.

Below: The crew of PD368 WS-A of IX Squadron pose with their battered aircraft after crashing on take off on 1 January 1945. The Lancaster was constructed in sections and the fuselage has broken at the joint between the rear and middle section. Note the thin yellow outline to the codes.

Of interest is the light coloured paint around the mid-upper turret coaming (arrowed). This is because PD368 took part in the sinking of the Tirpitz on 12 November 1944 (flown by Sqn Ldr 'Bill' Williams) and as it was an ultra long range op, the mid-upper turrets were removed to save weight.

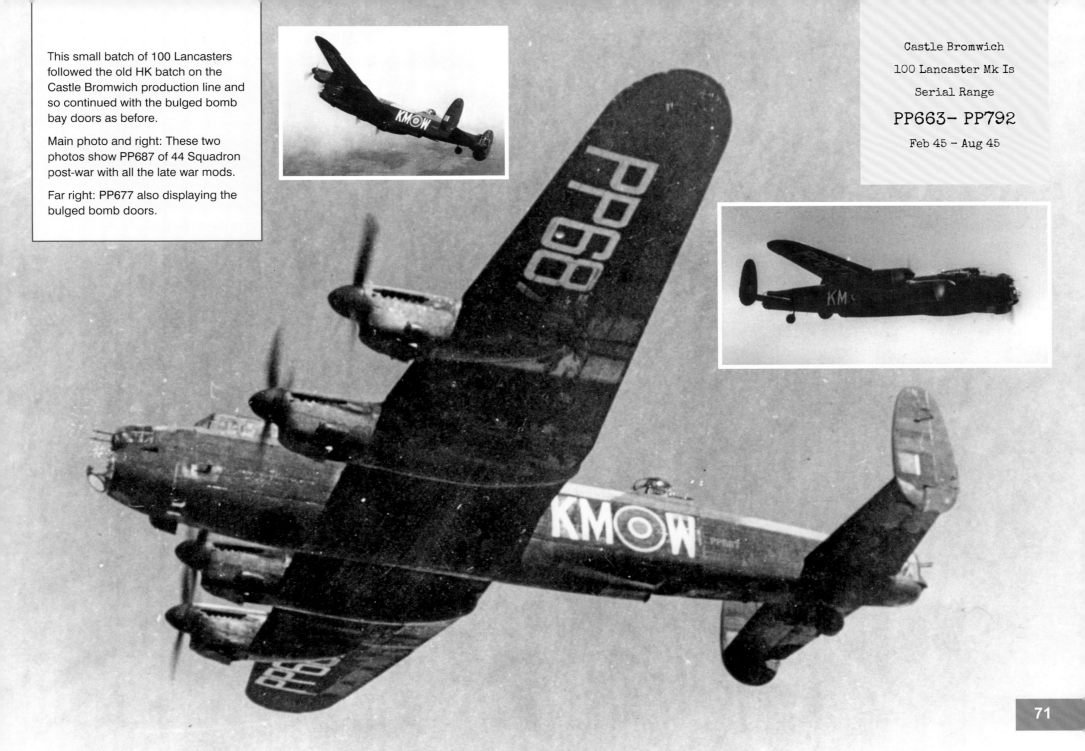

This small batch of 100 Lancasters followed the old HK batch on the Castle Bromwich production line and so continued with the bulged bomb bay doors as before.

Main photo and right: These two photos show PP687 of 44 Squadron post-war with all the late war mods.

Far right: PP677 also displaying the bulged bomb doors.

Castle Bromwich
100 Lancaster Mk Is
Serial Range
**PP663- PP792**
Feb 45 – Aug 45

Top: RA530 was delivered to 57 Squadron on 15 February 1945 and crashed on take off just over a month later. This shows that even in 1945, 5 Group tail markings were being applied to new aircraft.

Main photo and opposite: RA510 was a special aircraft as it was the 1000th Lancaster made by Metro-Vick. It was named 'Margaret' after Margaret Barber who was one of the factory employees and presumably the formidable woman standing by the port wheel on the opposite page!  Note that the Z-Equipment rings haven't been fitted yet.

By the end of the war, nearly half of Avro's employees were women, which has led to the often heard phrase in the north of England; *'my Nan worked on Lancasters!'*

This close up of RA510 shows the H2S mounting pole (A) clearly in the cockpit and the now completely black Rebecca aerials (B).

A.V. Roe (Yeadon)

87 Lancaster Mk IIIs

Serial Range

## RE115– RE226

Dec 44 – April 45

Above: RE172 provides ideal reference for the uppersurface camouflage pattern, virtually unchanged throughout the war. Note the later tall astrodome.

Top left: RE133 was delivered to 50 Squadron at the end of March 1945 and was scrapped a year later.

Left: This rare colour view of RE126 of 170 Squadron shows that this batch had the fuselage air intake fitted (arrowed).

Top: RF190 was delivered to 75 Squadron on 17 March 1945 and is photographed here six days later about to take of on a raid against Wesel. Of interest is the large whip aerial (arrowed) rarely seen in this position. Note the air intake (A) on the fuselage.

Above: QB-V is RF128, ex 424 Squadron seen here awaiting the scrapman. Having been left exposed to the elements, the perspex has started to discolour and the paint, especially the blue in the roundel, has faded significantly. Note the word 'Perspex' has been written on the H2S fairing.

Main photo: RF141 'Uncle Joe Again' awaiting the scrapman after the war. The white serial numbers under the wings were applied after the war ended to discourage pilots to indulge in low flying.

Inset left: A photo of RF141 shortly after delivery showing a more pristine appearance!

Inset right: One often overlooked feature of the very late war Lancasters is the removal of the port leading edge air intake (arrowed), mainly occuring on the those aircraft fitted with the fuselage air intake.

# LANCASTER Mk I RF141 JO-U 463 SQUADRON (MARCH 1945)

## Modeller's notes

Delivered to 463 Squadron on 22 February 1945

Merlin 24 engines
No fuselage windows
Paddle blade props
Late pitot tube
No H2S
Oval bomb aimer's window
No port cockpit blister
Z Equipment rings
Large astrodome
Rebecca Aerials
Fuselage air intake

Yellow outlined dull red codes with the U repeated on the outside of the fins.
Nose art 'Uncle Joe Again' with an image of Stalin on a red flag.*
*The original 'Uncle Joe', ED611, completed over 100 ops before being damaged beyond repair with 463 Squadron on 9 February 1945. RF141 was clearly named in its honour.

Survived the war

Right: A view of RF141's nose art, note the missing port leading edge air intake.

Just 37 examples were made in this batch but some did see action, hence their inclusion in this book.

Inset:  SW268 JO-R of 463 Squadron seen at Skellingthorpe in July 1945.

Main photo: This aircraft SW244 was fitted with an experimental saddle tank and long range navigation equipment to increase its range, in another experiment to enable Lancasters to operate in the Far East against Japan. The extra tank badly affected the handling when full so was not put into production.

Village Inn was the code name for the Airborne Gun Laying in Turrets (AGLT) system that was introduced in late summer 1944. Using the FN121 turret to house the equipment, a radar dish was connected to the guns so that it always pointed wherever the guns pointed. Using a Mk II Gyro Gunsight, and a set of cathode ray tubes and mirrors, AGLT projected a blip onto the gunsight to indicate where the approaching aircraft was, the blip was even given 'wings' to suggest the range.

The system still relied on the detected aircraft being hostile and so infra-red lamps (Z Equipment) were installed in the noses of all bombers to transmit a signal which could be checked by the gunner before opening fire.

Above Left: Rare colour stills of AGLT being demonstrated with the Perspex cover removed. Note how the dish points in the same direction as the guns at all times. Note also the port outer engine is running to provide hydraulic power for the rear turret for this demonstration.

Above: A close up of the radar dish enclosed in its dome which was only painted on the underside.

# Z-EQUIPMENT

One of the most distinctive of all Lancaster modifications during the second half of WWII was the addition of two circular rings in the bomb aimer's blister.  These were introduced in June 1944 and were infra-red signalling lamps that would flash a chosen code to indicate that the aircraft was friendly.  That flashing code would be visible to rear gunners who were equipped with an infra-red scope.  This scope was designed to be used with the Village Inn (AGLT) as seen on the previous page.

These rings were not factory fitted so can appear on even the earliest serial numbered Lancaster, if it survived beyond June 1944. The only clue they do give us is that any bomber carrying them must have been photographed after May 1944.